Explanations

Poems by Evelyn Klebert

Explanations
By Evelyn Klebert

A Cornerstone Book
Published by Cornerstone Book Publishers

Copyright © 2008 & 2024 by Evelyn Klebert

All rights reserved under International and Pan-American Copyright Conventions. No part of this book may be reproduced in any manner without permission in writing from the copyright holder, except by a reviewer, who may quote brief passages in a review.

First Cornerstone Edition - 2008
Second Cornerstone Edition – 2024

Cornerstone Book Publishers
Hot Springs Village, AR
www.cornerstonepublishers.com

ISBN: 978-1-93493-515-6

*For my husband,
my companion on my journeys,
I can't wait to see what's next.*

Love E.

Table of Contents

Footsteps of the Past 1
    Explaining 3
    Old Clothes 4
    An Unwanted Companion 5
    I remember 6
    Old Places 7
    Thrashing it Out 8
    Another Time 9
    Necessity 10
    A Picture 11
    Memories 12
    What's Left 13
    Sadness 14
    Children 15
    Old Wounds 16
    In Case 17
    If. 18
    Old Patterns 19
    I'm Sure 20
    Justice 21

Struggling Not to Backslide 23
    Certainty 25
    A Shallow Reflection 26
    Not Sure I Understand 28
    Climbing 29
    Chances 30
    Tearing 31
    Moody 32
    Listen 33

What's Worse?	35
A Shimmering	36
Pride	37
Virtuous	38
I Ran	39
The Unshakable	40
Whispers	41
Not So Easy	42
Stepping Stones	**43**
Me	45
Change	46
Little Gifts	47
A Misstep	48
A Different Voice	49
Something Elusive	50
That Time	51
Angels	52
What can I say?	53
Incidentals	54
Timing	55
A Gift	56
Grappling	57
Whims	58
A Blue Candle	59
Worry	60
Erosion	61
Closing In	62
What To Do	63
A Better Self	**65**
Your Voice	67
I Don't Have Time	68
The Moon	69
Stormy Waters	70

A Different Light 71
For Mom 72
A Rambling Road 74
The Fool 75
When 77
This Time 78
Milestones 80
Helping 81
Roads 82
Change 83
The Anchor 84
The Eye 85
Fireflies 86
The Mystery 87
Too Much Weight 88
How Much 89
Every Moment 90
They Don't Understand 91
So, I Release 92
Do You 93

Explanations

Footsteps of the Past

Explaining

Of course, I'm sure you'd like to know.
You'd like an explanation that serves you.
You'd like me to find words so that you can see
and fit this time quite neatly into your world.
You think I owe you a picture that will make sense,
One that your demeanor would deem acceptable.
You'd like an explanation,
I can still hear you saying,
You demand one, need one,
So, all that you believe can stay in place.
But I can't
And I won't,
And I probably never will.
So, your world cracks a little,
Just enough to let some light in.

Old Clothes

I wrestled with the past today,
like an old coat that didn't fit.
It scratched and rubbed my skin raw,
with tearing and untidy threads.
The garment had all but lost its shape,
simply an irritating echo of what once was.
The tangled threads no longer making sense,
only still around to remind me of old pain.
I wrestled with my past today,
then in a moment
I tossed it all away.

An Unwanted Companion

He is dressed in his finery,
a welcome consort.
One who will spin you adroitly
in twists and unexpected turns on the dance floor.
He will listen to your grievances, be a constant companion
if you so desire.
Fanning the flames of resentment, anger,
even blind and insane hatred if you wish to travel so far.
But if in a moment one can obtain distance,
and notice that the path traveled with this stalwart
companion makes no progress,
but wraps itself round in a deceptive circle.
Old ground disguised as new, is retread, old grievances
unhealed, and inflamed to infection.
He is a grand one, a compelling companion,
dressed in his finery disguised to please,
who keeps you a well-fed prisoner, well fed with poisons
that will only fester.
Poisons and wasted energy that would be better spent in
traveling with purpose, with progress,
beyond this particular horizon.

I remember

In a quiet moment,
In a blissful second,
I remember what has been,
and why I am.
I remember how I've been lost,
and how you gave me a place.
How I wandered,
and then how I knew where I should always be.
I remember how there is no one who makes me feel the center of the world.
No one who makes me feel as though my existence is paramount to them.
No one who makes me feel as though my thoughts, my words,
my heart, are rare treasures to their existence.
No one who makes me feel so essential,
as essential as you are to me.
And I remember why I am.

Old Places

What word or thought comes not from an old place?
Do we always view each other through the shades of the past?
Does a phrase trigger a memory, a slight,
a slander that makes us recoil not from the present
but from old pain?
It all seems like quicksand,
but are we ever truly be free or safe from such wounds?
Perhaps in freeing each other,
we free ourselves.
But then stand in our own vulnerability,
unguarded as we were the first time the daggers hit.
And the first tears were shed.

Thrashing it Out

Children are given a beloved sensibility.
They see the world through unsuspicious eyes,
unless they are taught suspicion.
They expect kindness from everyone,
unless they are taught cruelty.
Their nature is a trusting one,
unless their trust is broken.
As adults we carry the imprints from childhood,
sometimes more difficult to cast off,
than events experienced much later.
Like a footprint on freshly fallen snow,
that mars its pure essence.
So much care should be taken
in what we draw on that fresh new canvas.

Another Time

The mind is kind.

It gives us what we can absorb,

shields us from what cannot be handled.

It softens the harshness in memory,

filtering it through a gentler light.

It closes doors that should be left behind, but not completely,
not perfectly sealed.

So that when life is calmer, and the heart stronger

the door can be cautiously pried open.

And what was once intolerable,

can be revisited with a different perspective

Necessity

Sometimes when your world changes,
momentarily it goes unnoticed.
Life still runs you at a ragged pace,
and busyness moves you along from minute to minute.
Sometimes when the landscape shifts,
it's not readily taken in.
Your life is lived on schedule,
meshed from one event to the next.
And it's only when you finally stop,
reaching for a familiar signpost.
Your fingers stretched wearily, ready to grasp.
But it's not there, not where it should be.
Sometimes when your world changes,
you continue living in the old one,
until necessity makes that impossible.

A Picture

There is a picture that wraps around,
the past yet holds a key.
It seems what was, might be again
if only we could see.
It holds within its folds
a glimpse from another world.
The faces young, yet now are old.
The eyes untouched, by time or toil.
Such eyes, still brilliant, beckoning promise,
reminding us of possibility.
There is a picture that wraps around, what was,
and what will always be.

Memories

Memories grafted in fine little boxes,
set apart on a small dusty shelf.
Innocuous and quiet, and dormant they seem.
So separate from the wave of life, rushing about.
Were they ever a part of the life that's remembered?
Or just a dream swept away that no longer belongs.
Memories set distant in fine little boxes,
so forgotten and diffused,
they've all lost their toxin.
They've all lost their toxin.
Until they're breathed in
and that dust is brushed aside.
No longer so distant, no longer so separate.
No longer that dream that doesn't belong.

What's Left

The walls are white,
yet are smoky gray.
The windows clear,
yet smudged with dust and dirt.
The hallways empty,
yet cluttered with heavy footsteps.
The view is lovely,
yet marred by what was left.
The people have long gone,
but the house still holds all that's passed,
like a photograph that won't fade.

Sadness

It covers me like a drape.

Like a cloak that smothers energy, Smothers joy,

Smothers light.

It simply can't be closed,

Be close to what was pain.

I struggle with letting go,

Once I make peace,

There is only the next thing uncovered.

When is it at an end,

When does life move on again with peace, joy, hope?

How do I reconcile our past?

I can't even process it.

Children

When do we stop wanting validation,
a kind encouraging word, a pat on the back?
When do we stop needing their approval,
a murmur of praise, even when success isn't obvious?
When do we stop hoping for understanding,
even when years have passed
and there has never been an inkling.
When do we stop mourning the relationship
we think should have been,
and stop being pricked by the arrows of regret?
When do we accept them
for who they are and nothing more,
not who we wished they'd been,
but who they are?
Is there always time even in the twilight
to find a place to meet,
a common ground of peace?
Where we no longer seek,
but just recognize what is.

Old Wounds

Funny when you think it's all but said and gone,

when it seems the past has been tucked away in a neat, quiet, little corner, away from the present in a cage,

diluted of its venom.

Then a mere word, or look, or renewed acquaintance,

stirs the air.

And everything that seemed processed, that seemed dealt with, that had been put to rest, resurfaces with a vengeance,

in a wild tumult.

Causing one to wonder,

if wounds really ever heal,

and if we ever truly make peace

with that which has wounded us.

In Case

In case you didn't know,
Life comes in waves of bliss and strife,
In case you haven't seen,
Sometimes I'm queen,
And at other moments have no pride.
In case it wasn't obvious,
Peace doesn't come innately.
It's hard fought and hard won,
And often times leaves you friendless.
In case you didn't know,
I never claimed to know it all,
All I asked for occasionally was a little understanding.
I never thought I was better,
But oftentimes didn't follow the pack.
In case you haven't seen,
I'm probably nothing like what you think I am.

If

If I look at you through the filter of the past.
I only see what was.
If I focus on the mistakes you've made,
I trap myself next to you,
in pain,
in the past,
me that person who was hurt,
and you unthinkingly that person who hurt me.
If I triumphantly hang onto my wounds,
and won't release you from your affronts against me.
then we both are stuck in an ugly place,
where there is no hope for a better you or me.
If I look at you through the filter of the past,
I miss everything that you are now,
and that I have become.

Old Patterns

I'm not at all sure why, we can't just be.
Why we can't be quiet friends,
at this point in our lives.
Why we can't be friendly acquaintances,
just on the periphery of others' lives.
Why we can't co-exist in a peaceful way,
and let new times flower differently.
I'm not sure why the daggers still must fly,
why you feel the need to crush my little joys,
why you're still determined to hurt and demean
when things could be so different.

I'm Sure

I'm sure I knew them,
I had them pegged.
I watched them through a lifetime.
But now they change,
as swiftly as a breath,
leaving me quite wondering
if I ever knew them at all.

Justice

We're locked,

Like two mountain goats,

On a steep and barren crevice,

Locked, horns clashing,

Stirring occasionally,

A step here, a step there,

Trickles of old blood falling from the wounds,

The ones that we never allow to heal,

Just re-injure.

The sky above is not blue,

But gray with old, faded clouds rolling in.

Hard to remember how it began,

What offense was first,

Who drew first blood.

My muscles ache, and the time passes,

And passes,

And passes me by.

And I am so tired of it.

Think that you are right,
Walk away with your own validation,
But just end this and walk, walk away.
I yearn to see a different sky overhead.

Struggling Not to Backslide

Certainty

I cast a net into the ocean,
sure of what I'll catch,
but time and fate and winds of change
bring back the unforeseen.
I mark a page in my journal,
confident of what my life will bring,
but twists and turns and stumbles unknown
lead down an unexpected road.
I see myself in a passing glimpse,
in a mirror that has hung
forever it seems in the same place.
And I say to my image "Who will you be
when I look again tomorrow?"
Quite sure and quite confident
that I have no idea.

A Shallow Reflection

I prepare for attack,
arm myself for my nemesis,
readied for a long prepared-for battle,
guarded to the hilt to extremes.
Readied for the person who bears the brunt of my grievances,
who carries the burden,
the responsibility for my ills.
Readied for attack,
But then
you're here,
not as I've imagined,
not as I've armed against,
but beaten down and humbled by life,
eyes tired,
lined face,
sad from the heaviness of all the burdens yours and mine.
But where did my nemesis go?

The one I have prepared for, and armed against?
For my creation has dissipated as quickly,
as a reflection in shallow water,
rippling apart with a gentle breeze.

Not Sure I Understand

Not sure I understand
why when I've finally got everything together
it all seems to fall to pieces.
Not sure I understand why
that when I've run a hard race
and I think I'm finally done,
there's just another race around the corner.
Not sure I understand why
when I've finally unraveled that knot
the one that's plagued me for years,
at the bottom of the thread there's another
that's gone unseen
but seems twice as hard.
Not at all sure
why when I'm so ready to stop, and rest, and breathe,
there's only more to do,
no respite, no congratulations on a job well done,
but a new task wanting and needing all of me,
just waiting.
Not sure I understand why,
just that it goes and goes on.

Climbing

Some days seem dark,
and void of meaning,
wrapped in confusion and filled with missteps.
Others bring light,
and understanding,
a full grasp of what is and has been.
Progression tends to come in plateaus, periods of ascension,
then long, bleak spans of flailing that test us,
making us question and wonder if we are still climbing at all.

Chances

How many chances seem like enough?
How many times do we travel the same path?
How many arrows in our heart
feels a bit like one too many?
How deep is our capacity to forgive?
Then again, and again, and again...
What do you do with a turbulent child
that only seems intent on lashing out in pain?
A child with the face of an adult,
who should know better,
then again is there ever a cut-off for learning?
How many chances seem like enough?
I guess we'll find out.

Tearing

How fiercely we do cling,

to that thing we think we must have.

How fiercely we fight,

for that distant wish

that one that makes everything,

every choice,

every trade,

finally justified.

How valiantly, then wildly, then desperately we fight,

for things to be as we desire

as we imagine,

until it's finally ripped away,

completely, totally,

mercilessly and yet with great mercy.

Until we can finally see clearly

and without reservation

what was never there.

Moody

Walking down the moonlit pier,
drifting through the night.
Wondering why emotions fly,
then crash so abruptly in midair.
The air is humid,
my heart is heavy,
but I am sure it's only passing.
In the next moment,
or with the next sunrise,
all will be forgotten,
in the instant of a new thought.

Listen

Do you hear it wailing,
Fighting all the time?
It's always hungry,
Never filled, wanting, needing more.
It's a starving child in rags,
No matter how well you clothe it,
No matter how often you feed it.
It's never enough.
When you have all you ever wanted,
It wants something else.
When you are the center of attention,
And loved by so many,
It wants to be loved more.
When you find a place of peace and contentment,
It screams to a deafening pitch.
It begs you to explore aimless roads,
And stuff your life with gluttonies, nonessentials.
It knows no reason.

It lives on fear.

It's always alone no matter how well you comfort it.

I really don't know if the screaming child within us

ever truly leaves,

Ever truly grows up.

All we can do is love it, comfort it,

but like a good parent do what's best for it.

Not give in.

What's Worse?

Is it worse living through the perils of life?
Experiencing and breathing your own pain?
Is it worse looking from the inside out,
at a garbled perception filtered through upset?
Or is that easier than looking from the outside in,
trying to help but just falling short?
Is it worse as you silently watch the prelude to disaster build, knowing it,
but being helpless to stop the chain of events?

A Shimmering

We think we can predict,
what tomorrow will bring.
That what is familiar will still surround us.
We expect familiar smiles,
and voices on which we depend.
We use the yardstick of what has been
to stretch into the future.
No one's story can make us believe,
that we will not always be cushioned by what we anticipate.
It's only in that strange moment,
the one that departs and splits away from our world,
and remakes us,
that we see and know
how quickly in a shimmering that everything is changed.

Pride

I swallowed my pride,
Because life taught me it was expendable.
And watched while others insisted keeping theirs.
I swallowed my dreams so others could follow theirs,
Insisting that they were more relevant.
I sacrificed my life's path,
Because others felt mine was without consequence.
I bent myself to accommodate
Because others were louder with their desires.
I wiggled and molded until the mold broke,
Then I stopped,
And found myself again.

Virtuous

How do we convince ourselves that we are right?
We justify our actions in our mind.
How are we sure that our judgment is correct?
We supply our self with reasons to support our point of view.
How do we ensure that we haven't become self-serving?
We constantly remind ourselves
that we are doing what is for the best,
Even if it means interfering in someone else's life.
How do we know we haven't gone too far?
We reassure ourselves.
We convince ourselves.
We ignore the pain our actions cause.
How do we live with the consequences of our actions?
We lie to ourselves
And ignore the hatred we have created in others.

I Ran

I ran a marathon
Long and hard.
Pushing past limits,
Until not one inch of me didn't ache.
I ran like a pack of wolves
Were ravenous on my heels.
I ran from fear, from need,
From panic, and then I ran
To arrive quickly enough,
To move fast enough to please everyone.
But I was left with no breath.
And it was never enough.
I ran to help, and pushed
And pushed beyond limits but in the end
I fell short
And then fell apart.

The Unshakable

Some days are lofty,
and we hold tightly to our ideals.
It's easier to stay true,
When everything around is complacent.
But other times,
the wildness rips through,
And life shakes into a tumult,
Allowing no time for thought,
only for action.
But even then,
there is always the choice,
which way to go.
And how solidly in those moments
we can hang onto what we believe.

Whispers

Can you hear them,
When it's quiet?
Voices speaking softly.
Gently guiding,
Leading you along
To remember and See things clearly. Can you hear them
When the world is roaring?
When the noise of life
Becomes deafening?
Then it's so easy
To listen to louder voices,
Voices judging, pushing,
Demanding.
Can you see the difference
And where the difference leads?
One to peace, one to truth,
And the other spiraling down.

Not So Easy

I always believed peace would come easily.
It seemed like something natural that we're given
at birth, like sight or hearing.
But time and the rush of the world taught me
that it's not acquired so freely.
Oftentimes it's a struggle to find
and more so to keep.
It's an ongoing process
tested with each choice along the way.
A signpost, a traffic light,
directing which way to travel.
Sometimes not to the easier road
Or untroubled path,
But surely the one in the end
that will bring us home.

Stepping Stones

Me

I thought I knew quite distinctly who I was,

Was quite sure where my limits lie.

Could think and believe quite readily what space in this world I occupied.

My world seemed quite clear,

Not filled with shadows or secret places,

Not full but flat and predictable.

I thought that once,

That I knew.

But now what's most certain

Is that I did not.

Change

The sky is purple,
and the air is turbulent.
and the crack of change is thundering all about.
No one can tell what tomorrow will bring
or even the very next moment
for that matter.
But somehow, somewhere,
there is peace in knowing
a calm shore awaits if only within.

Little Gifts

Surprises and unexpected moments,
when you are sure all is predictable.
When the hours ahead and days stretch forward
with no anticipation,
a sudden unforeseen meeting.
An uncharted bend in the road
that gives just everything a new complexion.
A seed sown where ground was believed to be
infertile and barren.
Truly the mystery of life,
that place where hope springs up
exactly where it was thought to be impossible.

A Misstep

One of those days
when thinking becomes wrapped around a pole.
Crazy thoughts become sane in the filtered light,
and wild emotions look justified in the setting sun.
For that crazy moment,
the world tilts,
and danger lurks so close,
beckoning a rash, faltering, flawed decision.
One breath, one minute, one hour holding back
makes all the difference.
In one night's sleep calmness creeps in again,
sanity begins to balance perspective,
and thinking straightens out.
What a blessing,
just to wait,
wait to act,
before you send forward something that can't be taken back.

A Different Voice

All our lives we chase the dream,
that elusive thing we're sure will bring us happiness,
Wealth, success, admiration of strangers.
We strive and struggle and hope
that this will fill the dark void.
But the void only swallows,
and stretches,
and absorbs all the light.
In the darkness like a hungry child,
it cries more, and more and
more,
and never enough,
A ceaseless hunger,
Until fatigue and hopelessness takes us.
For how can never enough ever be quenched?
Perhaps a different path,
following a different voice,
where peace is never obtained at such a steep cost.

Something Elusive

A quiet breeze, yet something stirring the air
the calmness of the night,
seemingly serene, yet not peaceful.
Anticipation crackles, something elusive, prickling, irritating.
So close, yet just beyond reach,
brushing just near enough to drive us crazy with curiosity.
Something elusive, yet to be seen.

That Time

Difficult to judge,
not easy to tell.
When it's time to step back,
and allow things to go.
Allow them to drift away,
not truly understanding why.
But knowing it's all you can do,
that time to say goodbye.

Angels

A hush follows in their wake,
a rustle of wings,
a glimpse of light.
Perhaps it's a trick of the mind,
perhaps a wish imagined.
Perhaps we walk alone,
in silence,
in hollow silence,
and perhaps the gentle voices,
and whispers that cover us, surround, and bolster us
aren't there at all.
Aren't there to catch us when we stumble,
to inspire when we're empty.
Perhaps they aren't there,
but then again...

What can I say?

What can I say
when things go wrong?
What can I do
when the path is derailed?
How can I soothe the fears that sweep in
and let you know that the darkness isn't always?
What do I do
to let you know the world turns on a dime,
and in a breath it will turn again?
How do I help
when things go wrong?
Try and hope and find a way.

Incidentals

The nights are quiet,
the shadows long and twisting.
We walk a creaking staircase,
aware of steps uneven,
and unmeasured.
The landing is shaky,
but more stable as we walk deeper.
This hallway isn't nearly so dark,
as the one beneath us,
nor nearly so long.
And the end is in sight.
This is our house,
unexpected, not smooth, at times unsteady,
but strengthening.
This is our house.

Timing

When is it right to hold on tight?
To hold on with all your might?
And when is it right to loosen your grip,
and say a prayer as they walk away on such unsteady feet?
When is it time to watch them fly away,
to stand in awe as they soar,
reaching for the heights that you once dreamed about.
And when are you sure to stretch out your arms wide,
like you did when they took those sweet first steps.
To stretch your arms wide, so the fall won't be so rough,
so one day they won't be afraid to try again,
to reach upward for the stars,
for the dazzling heights.

A Gift

When vision clouds over,
and blindness sets in,
When the world wraps around you
in a tumultuous grip,
When everything seems tougher and harder
than it should,
Then sometimes a gift appears
unexpected.
Sometimes there is a shoulder
that helps shift the weight
from yours.
It is a treasure in disguise,
a kindness unparalleled.
An angel?
No, but then maybe yes.
A friend no more, no less,
a gift sent unexpected, but
so prized and so needed.

Grappling

Sometimes I yearn for solitude,
a bubble undisturbed,
away from things that shake my heart,
the life without such turns.
Surely peace shouldn't be so fragile, easily sabotaged by fate.
Surely calm should come from a stronger place,
not cast aside with the first great wave.
Sometimes I yearn for solitude,
but then life flowers in unexpected ways,
ways I'd miss if I were so set apart.
So instead, I try for a quiet place within,
that bends and yields within the storm,
a place of peace undisturbed,
that doesn't keep me distant and away,
but always, quite firmly anchors me.

Whims

Did you know

that we are so separate?

We think apart

and walk apart,

and desire things that seem worlds apart.

And yet the whims of one,

reverberate

like a splash in a vast pool.

It echoes onward,

rippling

continuously touching lives in ways we've never considered.

A Blue Candle

A blue candle burns on my desk late at night,
it wavers with indecision,
sometimes darker, sometimes light.
I hear nudgings and whispers,
from moments that have gone.
People who have walked near me,
then slipped away like phantoms
from some faraway dream.
The moment is quiet,
the spirit lost in solitude.
The meaning is indecisive,
but the candle continues to burn.

Worry

I worry about you
But I don't want to make it easier
If it's easier, you'll change nothing.
I feel your pain
But if I comfort too much
Your place of pain will feel softer,
More tolerable.
Am I cold to walk away?
And leave you to sort out your struggle.
Perhaps it's helping not giving You a soft place,
Forcing you to find a new one.
We all have to choose
But I worry that you won't.
That you'll go on in that dark place.
And if I let it,
my heart will break for you.

Erosion

Time tears down the wallpaper in soft slow shreds,
that show the wear gradually, imperceptibly.
Then all at once like a deluge,
as though all the undermining,
all the gradual erosion, didn't happen slowly,
but suddenly.
Except for those with watchful eyes,
who began to see the small cracks long ago.

Closing In

So close

So close to being able to draw breath

So close to being able to finally reach

reach the end, reach the summit, reach the finish,

only a stretch,

a stretch of fingertips.

And everything will be in place.

Will be done,

and then there will be rest.

Just one stretch,

one final stretch,

that only seems to stretch onward

just out of reach

endless.

What To Do

So overwhelmed,
As I watch lives spin out of control.
Was I delusional,
To believe I asserted any influence?
Should I sit back comfortably,
Or weep as I witness the destruction?
Is it some mad, bright, blinding star
Burning itself out of existence?
Could I just be mistaken,
And not have a clue at all?
Am I truly out of step with what is real
And true and pure?
So overwhelmed,
As I see others burn themselves out in a frenzy.
If they even wished to stop for a moment,
Would they even notice my outstretched hand?

A Better Self

Your Voice

I follow in silence.
I hear your voice.
It guides me through the darkness,
And through the chill of apathy.
I follow with hope,
Having all confidence that you will be there for me.
Knowing in this world of uncertainty you are my constant.
I listen quietly for your voice,
Knowing that if all was summed up of my life,
In a final word,
In a final whisper,
It would simply be,
"She loves him,
Always,
Always."

I Don't Have Time

I don't have time to dwell on past hurts,
To rage at the ones
Who hurt me.
I don't have the energy to plot my revenge,
And wish for grievances to be punished.
I don't have the will to keep the hate aflame,
It takes too much effort to fan that ugly fire.
I won't wish you ill,
Though at times I am tempted,
Because truly I know we are the authors of our own lives.
And we punish ourselves so much more than another could.
I won't spare the time to nurture old wounds,
There's too much else
All about that needs my efforts.

The Moon

I walked beneath the shining moon,
beneath its shimmering glow.
It led a path across the stillness,
that chilled me to the bone.
All truths I knew
fell into question,
beneath its luminescence.
All clarity blurred,
and certainty turned into whispers.
I stopped, entranced by its power,
wondering as my perceptions peeled away,
whether here, now, I had truly become lost,
or had finally found my way.

Stormy Waters

At times I fight what is,
thrash and claw and wish things were different.
More than sure there are easier choices,
choices that might lead me in a different direction.
At times I struggle against what I know is my road,
then I stop and breathe
deeply knowing it isn't in me to be anyone else.
So, I lay down my resistance and chart my course forward,
toward whatever it might bring.

A Different Light

What choice do I make,
when I turn away?
When I heed a different call.
Is it better to cling
or just let things gently float away
as the currents of life sweep us along.
I'm not so sure why it is,
that paths cross and touch,
sometimes just briefly.
And then what was needed is done,
and even as quickly,
lives bend toward a different light.
Is it a loss?
Or just the natural course of evolution?
When do we grip tight and hold on
and when do we recognize with clearness of vision
that time to let go?

For Mom

It's really hard to see,
through an infant's eyes,
the world around seems so confined.
But there are hands there to keep you safe,
a voice and arms
that teach this new world is truly filled
with kindness and love.
It's really hard to remember,
as the rush of living wants to sweep you along,
remember that somewhere there is an anchor,
a soul who continually gives more than it ever asks,
who takes joy and pride
in every step forward,
and comforts
through every fall.
It's easy to forget,
when your own life's dramas take center stage,
that there is always someone there,

watching, praying, hoping,
in your corner always.
Someone who doesn't seek anything,
but always celebrates your triumphs,
someone who always sees you as a blessing,
someone who truly is your blessing.

A Rambling Road

Down a rambling road,
when sunset is approaching,
I stop and look around,
and mark quite carefully,
where I have been.
The path behind leads me to this quiet respite,
and gives me ample time to look back.
Not now at specifics, nor incidents,
but only at the full arc of journey.
Now as I see it as a whole,
unbroken, and complete,
as I see it in the illumination of the setting sun,
it has a lovely flow and logic
that will fuel every step I take onward.

The Fool

I traveled in a dream,
I stumbled in a vision,
across a rocky terrain, unknown to me,
beneath a turbulent sky stretched wide with blue and white.
The man I met was not a stranger,
nor one I knew.
The place, it seemed, was more than familiar to him,
but he understood that I was a first-time explorer here.
He spoke but once, in curious words,
"The sky reaches downward and informs the earth."
His words, clearly riddles whose significance was lost on me.
So, I pushed onward.
The woman was next, regal yet serene,
Kind yet removed—eyes disturbingly cool,
like the reflection of the moon on a midnight ocean.
"You search too much,
the quest is not outward but within."
All seemed answered even before it was asked.

"We all travel together, but we all journey alone.
You can't choose for another,
nor can another make their choice
yours."
And then I knew, as though by insight,
If I walked forward, it would be into the world,
outside the realm of these truths,
but carrying them, integrated
somehow.
I did not feel myself the Fool,
but instead, an initiate,
a learner upon the untried path of the Fool.

When

When does a mystery yield its secrets?
Not on my clock,
not on my time,
when I demand it do so.
Pushing, and pulling,
and trying to force its lock.
When will a shadow find its way to sunlight?
Not when I deem it is far past sunrise,
not when I expect it is time for it to do so.
When will a seed planted finally bloom into full flower?
Not by predictions of experts,
not by forecasts of weather.
but when and only when the seasons shift,
boding a full and imminent change.

This Time

Those quiet times we forget,
we simply move on as if we were alone.
The path glides easily,
and so life takes hold,
with its busyness
that fills the days.
Those other times,
stormy times,
when chaos is rampant,
and confusion blocks our view.
Then we remember,
frantically reaching out our hands to be be guided,
supported, simply helped through.
When it all seems too much,
we desperately, readily shift the burden,
remembering that there is always someone there
to take it from us.
With assurance that even if we don't understand,

we are loved and cared for and never truly alone.
In time the darkness will lift,
and again, life will go on easily,
but perhaps this time we'll remember
and consider who led us to the other side.

Milestones

Quiet milestones,
mark the road.
Not bright, or bold,
not flashy, or earth shattering,
but silent and steady.
Some missed, overlooked,
not looked upon at all until you're looking backward.
A memory, an old photo,
a smile once forgotten,
that says simply and serenely,
everything's changed from this moment on,
and nothing, definitively,
nothing will ever be the same.

Helping

I'm not sure where I can help most.
I'm not sure the best thing to do.
Perhaps I'll sit back and watch and wait,
For a clue, a trail,
something that marks my way.
I'm not sure the best way to help.
You won't tell me the truth,
But only what you think I want to hear.
So instead, I'll listen to the unspoken words,
And piece it together the best that I can.
It's a guess at most,
A feeling, an instinct, that's all I have,
All I have and the best I can do.

Roads

I wasn't sure this morning,
which way I might be traveling.
The sun beckoned to me, a lovely, welcoming path,
so bright it was difficult to see much in the distance.
This road would be a new one, uncharted by the past.
In the other direction,
lay the place I had been before.
Not so bright, not so welcoming,
but surely safe and guarded well by experience.
The question was surely what sort of travel would I take.
Would I walk to the unknown
but where possibility paved the way,
or would I re-tread where it was safe and comfortable,
but nothing new would be learned?
So, as I set off this morning,
the choice didn't seem a choice at all.
For aren't we all explorers
placed here as students in this life and of this world?

Change

Change comes on a whisper with the breeze,

like a tantalizing thread that quietly wraps around

your hands.

It beckons,

and leads you gently along a different course.

Change comes like a crashing wave unexpected, devastating,

invigorating.

It wipes clean what was foreseen, stripping the landscape

bare.

Making way for life to flourish once again.

The Anchor

How can your world change

in a moment, a simple breath?

What seems solid and dependable

simply slips away as though it were a phantom.

All its simple, dependable expectancies shimmer

into a memory.

Leaving you wondering where at all is solid ground.

In a moment your world bends in on itself,

remolding and remaking in unrecognizable ways.

You become the anchor around which all else

reforms itself.

You are its constant,

against which the waves crash.

The Eye

There's a place outside of the storm,

or inside if you prefer.

It's an odd view,

somewhat unobstructed,

ever so slightly removed from the chaos, from the franticness, from the rampant delirium.

It's a calm perspective, where vision is cleared, and profound thoughts are borne.

Fireflies

Illuminating the darkness
with an eerie glow,
they flash and dart,
appearing near and far,
jaggedly across the air.
The quiet stirs,
the blackness ebbs,
and their illuminations track across
a slowly awakening sky.
They point us toward morning,
which arrives desperately anticipated,
but never,
never as quickly as we would desire.

The Mystery

I'm not sure why you stepped into our lives,
brought with you an energy,
a brightness that reminded us to live,
live with energy, with joy, with brightness.
I'm not sure why you chose to come our way,
to bring a sweetness into the darkest of times.
How you graced us,
and then you left.
I'm not sure why,
but even as we missed you,
we felt that cool sweet breeze
when you opened the door to leave.
The one that reminds us of what will be.
I'm not sure why you had to go,
but I do know we are better for the time you were with us.

Too Much Weight

I woke up this morning,

Busy with things to do,

Hurrying into a day filled to the brim.

I woke up this morning

And moved more quickly

With a lighter heart, and a mind free of burdens.

I woke up this morning and completely forgot.

Forgot I had grievances,

Forgot I was angry,

Forgot all the things I've been holding against you.

And then I remembered,

But realized how all that effort at being angry

Weighed me down,

As though I was dragging around

A bundle of useless, cumbersome weights,

That took so much effort to create

And sustain.

So, I left them behind,

Releasing you, but much more so Releasing myself.

How Much

How does God want us to help each other?
How much or how little do we do?
How much becomes too much?
How little becomes not enough?
What is the best help?
Doing or not doing?
And when do we know the difference?

Every Moment

If I could give one moment in time
Away,
exchanged for a simpler life.
I wouldn't know which one to pick,
Because no matter how hard the climb,
No matter how painful at times,
No matter how difficult
And treacherous the road.
It always led me back to you,
And so, every moment spent on that trip,
Was worth where I am now.

They Don't Understand

I can't explain why they can't see as I do.

I can't begin to explain why things are as they are.

I can't explain why my life is drawn the way it is.

I can't make you understand why my heart is wrapped with yours.

I can't explain why I know where I must be,

And that there is a great gift in knowing.

I can't help it that they don't agree.

I can't make them understand why my whole life is about loving you.

It is

It simply is.

So, I Release

So, I release judgment
Because it's not mine to give
And so, I release anger
Because it's a poison I don't wish to carry.
So, I release worry
Because it accomplishes nothing
And so, I release guilt
Because we all choose our own direction.
And so, I release fear
Because it casts shadows where they shouldn't be.
And I wake to a brand new day.

Do You

Do you remember who I am,
Who I was dancing in the rain.
Who I am listening for your voice,
Who I was dreaming about what would be,
Who I am tending to our lives,
Who I was daring the fates to stop me,
Who I am remembering who I was.

More Books by Evelyn Klebert

The Lady in the Blue Dress
6 x 9 Softcover & Hardcover 214 pages
ISBN 978-1-61342-600-5
ISBN (Hardcover) 978-1-61342-418-6

When she was a child, Mika Devalieur was introduced to her grandmother's most precious possession — a priceless and mysterious painting that she simply called The Lady in the Blue Dress. Upon Adele St. Clair's death, the painting is left in the care of her granddaughter with only one stipulation. Mika must hand over the family heirloom to a total stranger. Mika Devalieur desperately wants to deny her beloved grandmother's last request, but she can't. Torn between her Gran's last wishes and her desire to hold onto the Lady, she ultimately journeys to rural Virginia, where an enigmatic man shows her that this painting is only the beginning.

What quickly becomes clear is that James Clairmont knows much more about her and the Lady than he is letting on. He begins to slowly unravel a powerful supernatural connection that spans three generations of her family. Mika finds herself desperate to uncover the entire truth before she falls in love with a man filled with so many secrets — secrets about him, about her, and most especially about The Lady in the Blue Dress. (First published on Kindle Vella, episodes 1-23.)

More Books by Evelyn Klebert

Dumaine Street
6 x 9 Softcover & Hardcover 306 pages
ISBN 978-1-61342-902-0
ISBN (Hardcover) 978-1-61342-416-2

Voices in her head, catastrophic emotions, hallucinations – Rebecca Wells is more than convinced that she is losing her mind. And as a last-ditch effort, she contacts a self-professed counselor who seems convinced he can help.

Gabriel Sutton has abandoned the world of medicine to navigate a realm filled with psychic phenomena. Diagnosing Becca with extreme empathic abilities, he struggles to help her stabilize her gifts while trying desperately not to fall in love with his patient.

From the realm of vulnerability into a crusade to use their profound gifts to rescue others from peril on the other side of death, these two follow an astonishing and unpredictable path into each other's hearts.

The Tethering
A Portent of Crows
6 x 9 Softcover & Hardcover 201 pages
ISBN 978-1-61342-599-2
ISBN (Hardcover) 978-1-61342-419-3

Deborah Brandt's beloved Aunt Gena always told her that she was special, a bit different, and would have to live her life, unlike other people. Of course, this she disregarded as the ramblings of her lovely but notably eccentric aunt. Although there were the things that Aunt Gena said that seemed true — like Deborah being sensitive to energy shifts, having potentially psychic impressions, and dreaming of a spirit guide

— none of it could be real. But the most ridiculous thing that her Aunt Gena told her before she died was that someone special was out there for her. She said that he was an extraordinary man who was not only her perfect match but someone who she would learn from so that they could help the world in difficult times. How ridiculous! It sounds like a fairy tale, and no such person exists.

Daniel Wren is unique. He has been raised and trained from a young age to hone his psychic gifts. He lives in a world unimagined by most. And he has been waiting for years to contact his counterpart, soulmate, if you will. But the problem is that she is painfully unaware of the type of life that he lives and the life she would be entering into if they came together.

His dilemma becomes how best to proceed. How can he win her over and move forward before outside forces take that decision away from him?

Travels into the Breach
Accounts of a Reluctant Mystic
6 x 9 Softcover & Hardcover 171 pages
ISBN 978-1-61342-323-3
ISBN (Hardcover) 978-1-61342-417-9

At first glance, his life seems quiet, serene, and even uneventful. Malachi McKellan, a 65-year-old widower and author of esoteric books, lives largely as a recluse in a house situated just off the banks of Bayou St. John in New Orleans. But unbeknownst to most, he is also a bit of a detective, a specific kind of detective whose specialty is psychic attacks. Alongside his lifelong companion and spirit guide Simon Tull, a 19th-century, 20-something English gent, Malachi battles the unseen, and is an unacknowledged hero to the most vulnerable. Most of the population have no idea what is really happening beneath the surface of the world in which they live.

In this collection of adventures, Malachi McKellan and Simon Tull wage war against the most insidious elements of the paranormal. In *The Three*, Malachi and Simon come to the aid of a young woman being victimized by a group of dark witches. An old apartment building is the scene of an unimaginable battle against monstrous forces in *The Lost Soul*. Malachi and Simon find themselves strategizing against a psychic vampire in *Obsession*, and *The Hotel* turns back time to the 1980s where Malachi confronts a demonic spirit. In *Between*, a past life is revisited as Malachi attempts to rescue a beloved sister from committing her existence to vengeance, and *The Wedding* takes a personal turn when Malachi must confront painful truths while endeavoring to protect his niece from a potentially devastating union.

Travel into the breach with a pair of paranormal warriors who choose to confront overwhelming forces on a battlefield unsuspected by most.

Gravier's Bookshop
A New Orleans Paranormal Mystery (#1)
6 x 9 Softcover & Hardcover 172 pages
ISBN 978-1-61342-288-5
ISBN (Hardcover) 978-1-61342-411-7

Max Gravier had no intention of becoming a recluse, but after his wife's death it seems his life is heading in that direction. He spends his time running Gravier's Bookshop on Magazine Street and occasionally on the quiet helps the police solve a crime with his psychic sensitivities. That is until he answers Caroline Breslin's call, a cry for help out of his dreams that draws him into a fierce battle for a young woman's soul.

In this first installment of The New Orleans Paranormal Mystery series, Caroline Breslin, an amazingly gifted empath, is determined to strike out on her own and has moved out from the protection of her family home. All is going extremely well until, of course, she comes under siege from a devastating supernatural attack. The last thing Caroline wants is to run back to her family for help, even though she is painfully in over her head. What she really needs is a knight in shining armor — or maybe just that guy that keeps haunting her dreams.

Join them and the whole Breslin family psychic clan in this first installment of The New Orleans Paranormal Mystery Series where you'll travel into a new world just a few steps into the turbulent realm of the unseen.

The Hotel Mandolin
A New Orleans Paranormal Mystery (#2)
6 x 9 Softcover & Hardcover 146 pages
ISBN 978-1-61342-290-8
ISBN (Hardcover) 978-1-61342-412-4

Peril is wrapped up in the most enticing of disguises in *The Hotel Mandolin*, the second installment of The New Orleans Paranormal Mystery series. It's opulent, classic, and one of the most renowned hotels nestled deep in New Orleans' famous business district, but something is amiss at The Hotel Mandolin.

PI Peter Norfleet is calling out the big guns to help him investigate a recent suicide at the famous establishment — his good friend Max Gravier, a formidable psychic, and his girlfriend, Caroline Breslin, a talented empath. But none of them can seem to scratch the surface of this puzzle, no one except Cassie Breslin, Caroline's clairvoyant mother, who has somehow tapped into an unexpected connection with a tragic ghost from the turn of the century. And the more she uncovers, the more dangerous and malevolent the mystery becomes

The House at Pritchard Place
A New Orleans Paranormal Mystery (#3)
6 x 9 Softcover & Hardcover 138 pages
ISBN 978-1-61342-292-2
ISBN (Hardcover) 978-1-61342-413-1

Nothing is really wrong with the old Warrick House on Dante St. except that there most certainly is. Nothing is exactly wrong with its new mysterious owner except that Elise is sure that something doesn't add up. It isn't obvious, but sometimes the most dangerous things aren't.

In the third installment of The New Orleans Paranormal Mystery series, with the help of her very psychic sister and her children, the Breslin clan, Elise Ashford is about to embark on a wild rescue mission straight into another dimension that will land her squarely somewhere she doesn't expect, right back into her past. She'll land full circle; in a childhood home whose memory still haunts her to this day -- *The House at Pritchard Place.*

More Books by Evelyn Klebert

Treading on Borrowed Time
6 x 9 Softcover & Hardcover 223 pages
ISBN 978-1-61342-214-4
ISBN (Hardcover) 978-1-61342-436-0

For Julia Moreau, life seems complicated. Emerging from a failed marriage and managing a lifetime of diabetes, she lives alone in her childhood home where she communicates with the spirit of her Great Aunt Lilia. But Julia doesn't have a clue what complicated is until she is thrust into being the key chess piece in a match between two powerful men of extraordinary abilities on the wild hunt for a mystical creature hidden in the heart of New Orleans' French Quarter. Will Julia lose her soul to the karma of a devastating past life or her heart to the love of a man driven by dark forces? What is clear is that whichever way she turns she is *Treading on Borrowed Time*.

Sanctuary of Echoes
6 x 9 Softcover & Hardcover 371 pages
ISBN 978-1-61342-211-3
ISBN (Hardcover) 978-1-61342-409-4

Ghosts unacknowledged do not sleep.
Corey Knight has resigned herself to a quiet, reclusive life spent living out the rest of her days in her childhood home on the fringes of New Orleans' French Quarter. But the unexpected specter of her deceased father plunges her into a mad quest for a missing supernatural weapon unearthed long ago. And unfortunately, her only ally is a lost love she once betrayed.
Iain Shaw returns to New Orleans, a city he abandoned a decade before while fleeing a devastating past. Here, he is

forced to confront it again in the visage of the woman he once adored - one that he is now determined to get back at any cost.

Follow them both in a wild paranormal tale of discovery and redemption as they confront and unearth the echoes of a buried and unyielding truth that once tore them irreparably apart.

A Quiet Moment
6 x 9 Softcover & Hardcover 273 pages
ISBN 978-1-61342-326-4
ISBN (Hardcover) 978-1-61342-435-3

Jacob Wyss is caught in a rut, in fact on the verge of being engulfed by it. After an excruciating and disillusioning divorce, his life as an artist in a sleepy-college town at the foot of the Appalachian Mountains has become quiet, routine, and maddening in its predictability. One wintry day, his deep restlessness drives him out in precarious conditions to a largely empty bookstore nearly devoid of another living soul, nearly.

Aimee Marston isn't like everyone else. On the surface, she lives a sedate life working as a feature writer for a small local newspaper in addition to several other editorial jobs to help make ends meet. But just beneath, her existence is largely not her own. She is a sensitive, an empathetic psychic, guided by her calling to use her gifts to help others. Unfortunately, as a result, her secretiveness has made her defensive, protective of herself, and prevented her from having much of a life.

A psychic call for help sends Aimee out on a freezing January morning where her destiny and Jacob's collide sending both their lives spiraling onto an unexpected and often disturbing track. Two lonely souls connect, not by accident, but by design. Theirs is the intersection of two spiritual paths, two

More Books by Evelyn Klebert

lovers who must struggle to overcome the phantoms of a past life, as well as the challenges of their own inner demons to carve out an extraordinary future together.

A Ghost of a Chance
6 x 9 Softcover & Hardcover 230 pages
ISBN 978-1-61342-162-8
ISBN (Hardcover) 978-1-61342-440-7

You never know what's coming next.

Jack Brennan, an ambitious high-powered attorney, dies. But that's not the end, rather only the beginning. He finds himself constrained to an inexplicable afterlife as an earth-bound spirit trapped in an old Virginia farmhouse. His only companion is a very much living, reclusive writer of campy vampire novels. The maddening problem is that Hallie does not know he is there, nor that he is somewhat reluctantly falling in love with her.

Hallie Barkly is recovering from a painful and disillusioning divorce. Out of the ashes of her former life, she has managed to somehow forge a career and exorcise her demons by writing under the pseudonym of Sebastian Winters. Slowly, she is awakening to the fact that she is not alone.

Their lives intersect, and two unconventional lovers are brought together under insurmountable circumstances. Together they must battle an unseen force hell-bent on possessing Hallie's life and bridge death itself to make possible what cannot be — to find a chance.

More Books by Evelyn Klebert

Dragonflies - Journeys into the Paranormal
6 x 9 Softcover & Hardcover 176 pages
ISBN 978-1-88756-072-6
ISBN (Hardcover) 979-8-32548-418-6

In every form of creation, there is a blueprint for living, for experience, for interpretation. In flight, they can twist, turn, alter direction, pause in midair, and even fly backward. The dragonfly is the master of adaptability. They are a living prism, refracting light, and color, seemingly shifting their essence.

The lesson the dragonfly gives is that life is never what it appears to be.

In "The Wizard," as a novice practitioner of magic, Aurora Finn finds herself battling against the illusions of a powerful wizard intent on separating her from the world she knows. "The Sojourners" is a gentle story of a mother and daughter whose tenancy in an old Virginia farmhouse uncovers the trials and sorrows of its former occupants. A bookstore clerk gets an extraordinary customer on Halloween night in "Late One Night at Berstrums Books." In "The Tear," a woman coping with her fatal illness unknowingly begins a track on a mystical journey that will entirely restructure her vision of the world.

These stories follow the path of the dragonfly imbued with the momentum and energy of change, taking a winding and treacherous journey that ultimately leads to truth buried beneath perception.

More Books by Evelyn Klebert

Breaking Through the Pale
6 x 9 Softcover 134 pages
ISBN 978-1-88756-045-0

Journey with metaphysical author Evelyn Klebert into a collection of short stories that travel beyond the pale into the unpredictable realm of the paranormal.

In "A Grey Mourning," a disillusioned man encounters a mysterious being on the foggy streets of New Orleans. "Contact" is a tale of automatic writing, when a young artist establishes communication with a spirit guide, and the victim of a car crash unravels the true nature of her existence in "Dancing on the Threshold." The final tale is called "Isolation," in which a confused and disoriented woman finds herself in an old, quaint house where she must piece together the mystical implications surrounding her predicament.

The Witches' Own
6 x 9 Softcover & Hardcover 140 pages
ISBN 978-1-61342-058-4
ISBN (Hardcover) 978-1-61342-428-5

On the surface things seem quiet and serene in the picturesque coastal village of Kilmarnock, Virginia. But something unseen roams its lush forests as the past and present collide and the unthinkable begins to wreak its vengeance. Young Lucy Bonner is executed for witchcraft in the town's distant and brutal past. Her death triggers an unholy chain of events which grasp at the restless heart of novelist Peter McQuade, spurring him towards a quest to uncover the dark and terrifying truth.

More Books by Evelyn Klebert

The Left Palm
And Other Halloween Tales of the Supernatural
6 x 9 Softcover & Hardcover 122 pages
ISBN 978-1-93493-556-9
ISBN (Hardcover) 978-1-61342-442-1

Halloween is the time of year when that veil between worlds is thinned, and you can just catch a quick glimpse into the realm of the unknowable. In this collection of short stories, Evelyn Klebert takes you to a place where ordinary life splinters into the sphere of the paranormal.

The journey begins with one woman's unstoppable quest for vengeance against a supernatural creature in "Wolves" and continues in an old historical graveyard where a horrifying discovery is uncovered in "Emma Fallon." In "The Soul Shredder," a psychiatrist's unusual patient opens his eyes to a disturbing new view of reality, while in "Wildflowers," a woman strikes up a supernatural friendship with impossible implications. And in "The Left Palm," a fortuneteller in the French Quarter receives a most unexpected and terrifying customer.

White Harbor Road
And Other Tales of Paranormal Romance
6 x 9 Softcover & Hardcover 152 pages
ISBN 978-1-61342-066-9
ISBN (Hardcover) 978-1-61342-441-4

A psychic soul mate, a time traveler, a horror writer, and an enigmatic stranger take a selection of resilient, life-battered heroines to a place of paranormal healing and transformation.

More Books by Evelyn Klebert

In this collection of short stories, *White Harbor Road* is the last stop where life's burdens and hardships evolve into something unexpected.

The Broken Vow
Vol. I of The Clandestine Exploits of a Werewolf
6 x 9 Softcover & Hardcover 204 pages
ISBN 978-1-61342-133-8
ISBN (Hardcover) 978-1-61342-420-9

In the heart of every man there is a history. In the heart of every monster there is a story. In this first installment of *The Clandestine Exploits of a Werewolf*, Ethan Garraint is on a vendetta that begins in the heart of the Pyrenees with the fall of Montségur and leads him to the streets of New Orleans nearly five hundred years later. But the person he chases isn't really a man anymore and Ethan has been a werewolf for almost a millennium. With the aid of a gifted seer, he is on a blood hunt that will culminate in a journey that crosses the line between heaven and earth and ends somewhere in between.

Considerations
6 x 9 Softcover 84 pages
ISBN 978-1-88756-062-7

Sometimes the struggle to understand the meaning and complexities of living comes down to a single moment of introspection or a fleeting yet meaningful reflection. This collection of poetry by Evelyn Klebert takes you down a winding path of self-discovery where the resolution may not always be absolute, but the journey is indeed unforgettable. It

More Books by Evelyn Klebert

a wide and varied map of inspired poetry for your examination and consideration.

Appointment with the Unknown
The Hotel Stories
6 x 9 Softcover & Hardcover 155 pages
ISBN 978-1-61342-360-8
ISBN (Hardcover) 978-1-61342-421-6

A hotel, for most, represents a normal place, a predictable realm of commonality. One might even go as far to say a safe space, the reliable where nothing particularly unusual is expected to happen. Or is it? Dimensional traveling, spirit guides, mystical storms, and soul mates separated by time are only a few elements dotting this supernatural landscape. Drop into a collection of romantic paranormal stories where that place of commonality is only the threshold, the jumping-off point, for extraordinary adventures into the unknown.

Visit Evelyn's website at:
www.evelynklebert.com

Cornerstone Book Publishers
www.cornerstonepublishers.com

www.ingramcontent.com/pod-product-compliance
Lightning Source LLC
LaVergne TN
LVHW041339080426
835512LV00006B/539